BREATHING AIR

OF LOVE, HEARTBREAK, AND JOY

RASHI ARORA

For all the believers of love out there!!

Explore till you meet your better half,
Then love as you've never before.

Contents

Foreword *ix*

1. A Beautiful Ride 1
2. A Painting 2
3. Acting And Acing 3
4. Alright 4
5. Anytime But Tomorrow 5
6. Back Then 6
7. Biking And Hiking 7
8. Breaking Away 8
9. Breathing Air 9
10. Cats And Dogs 10
11. Coffee And Bread 11
12. Don't Go 12
13. Dream Man 13
14. Drug Of Love 14
15. Easy Or Tricky 15
16. Enough Theft 16
17. Eros 17
18. Everything Right 18
19. Expectation 19
20. Eyes & Love 20
21. Fighting The Mess 21
22. From The Shelf 22
23. Good Times 23

Contents

24. Grim 24

25. Gripped 25

26. Home 26

27. I Will Meet You 27

28. Ignore And Focus 28

29. Illusion 29

30. Merry-go-round 30

31. Just A Try 31

32. Letter 32

33. Loveless 33

34. In The Garden 34

35. Musical Tones 35

36. North- South 36

37. Rainbows 37

38. Roses And Thorns 38

39. Seedling To Bloomed 39

40. Seesaw 40

41. Someday 41

42. Swifty 42

43. Tattoo 43

44. The Way To You 44

45. True Or False 45

46. Truth Or Myth 46

47. Twenty- One 47

Contents

48. Valley Of Emotions 48

49. You 49

50. Your Sweetheart 50

Foreword

It’s all about the feelings we feel.

Whether it is Love, Joy, or Heartbreak.

1. A BEAUTIFUL RIDE

Meeting you was,
Not just a coincidence.
It is a beautiful ride,
And I don't want to depart.
I keep tossing and turning,
Till I hear the alarm ring.
Roaming around without stubbing the toe,
Like walking on a layer of snow.
Meeting you was,
Not just a coincidence.
It is a beautiful ride,
And I don't want to depart.
Eyes full of light,
Smiling just right.
Hairs did like a pro,
And Emotions in a rhythmic flow.
Meeting you was,
Not just a coincidence.
It is a beautiful ride,
And I don't want to depart.

2. A PAINTING

As if you were a painting,
So deep and unreal!
Had your Eyes Lined with emotions,
Which the lips were ready to speak!
Cheeks hinted with the rosy blush,
The ears listen to the wind gush.
Looking at that is a face like
Looking at a masterpiece.
Looking at those strides,
I don't want you away from my sight.
I want to stay by your side,
Till the end of day and night.
From the lows to the highs,
Where everything is bright.
As if you were a painting,
So deep and unreal!

3. ACTING AND ACING

Oh! how I knew you were acting,
All this time in the fall and spring.
Like the time you drove,
I developed so much hope.
As if I was not only a toy,
And you played with joy!
The time we went to see the racing!
And you were acing,
Just in spite of continuing to humiliate,
In the restaurant, we ate.
Tracing through all those days,
With tears falling on my face.
Oh! How I knew you were acting,
All this time in the fall and spring.

4. ALRIGHT

Hand in hand,
Walking around the beach,
Leaving behind a trail.
With the dog following without a leash.
Laughing as the waves hit,
Next to the firepit.
Even when the teeth grit,
And sides tickled.
Hand in hand,
Walking around the beach,
Like behind a trail,
With the dog following without a leash.
With you by my side,
I can even conquer a tide.
It's alright,
Everything's alright.

5. ANYTIME BUT TOMORROW

As the pages turn yellow,
I realized anytime but tomorrow.
Trying to end the wait,
I fight with my fate.
Tears falling for you,
Hoping to meet, to see you.
In the daily chaos,
I still hope.
Sobbing over the broken promise,
Thinking about your demise.
As they finished the war,
You turned into a star.
As the pages turn yellow,
I realized anytime but tomorrow.
Trying to end the wait,
I fight with my fate.

6. BACK THEN

I am standing alone,
And you are gone.
I am still of that time,
Back then when you were mine.
Sharing coffee cups,
And kisses and hugs.
Talking through sleepless nights,
Looking at the starlit night.
I am standing alone,
And you are gone.
I am still of that time,
Back then when you were mine.

7. BIKING AND HIKING

Oh! How I miss the days,
Before we went separate ways.
When we went hiking,
Along with some biking.
The days of love ended,
The letters of love are unattended.
I Never got to ask,
Was my love only a task?
Eating with from you,
To scooting away from you.
I remember the days and nights,
Of fake smiles and fights.
Oh! How I miss the days,
Before we went separate ways.
When we went hiking,
Along with some biking.

8. BREAKING AWAY

Things were fatal,
In the breaking away scandal.
It became natural,
Just like a falling petal.
Searching hopes,
Broken bones.
Hopes for breath,
Oh! the breaking away aftermath.
God has played their move,
With us hoping to be rescued.
Trying to break away from life,
Still watching that knife.
Things were fatal,
In the breaking away scandal.
It became natural,
Just like a falling petal.

9. BREATHING AIR

To this day,
Sitting on the chair.
Looking at you,
Is as easy as breathing air.
Afraid to take a step,
Avoiding any misstep.
Hoping that talking to you,
Is as easy as breathing air.
Till this day
Want to walk along with you
Hoping that
It is as easy as breathing air.

10. CATS AND DOGS

Was it for a pencil?
Or using an eraser.
Standing in the front,
Or dating the player?
Oh, how it turned,
From fighting like cats and dogs.
To be showered,
In the love of yours.
Locking eyes in the library,
Running to the stationery.
Fixing strands of hair,
And touching here and there.
Oh, how it turned,
From fighting like cats and dogs.
To be showered,
In the love of yours.

11. COFFEE AND BREAD

More than sipping coffee,
And sharing bread.
You keep stitching,
My life with rainbow threads.
Both of us fighting,
Alongside and opposite.
In the parade,
Or on the flavor of the icing.
More than sipping coffee,
And sharing bread.
You keep stitching,
My life with rainbow threads.

12. DON'T GO

Don't go!
If only you can know,
The feeling I feel,
I know how I conceal.
I'm losing all the scope,
You're my only hope.
Life is turning like a daily soap,
And I don't know the trope.
Don't go!
If only you can know,
The feeling I feel,
I know how I conceal.

13. DREAM MAN

Features like a tonic,
To get drunk on.
Physique so fine,
I just want to lean on.
It's all about the dream man,
But it's all spam!
Curated with kindness,
Everything is about carefulness!
Features like a tonic,
To would get drunk on.
Physique so fine,
I just want to lean on.
Maybe this,
Or go for that.
In the end,
It's all written beforehand!

14. DRUG OF LOVE

I didn't knew the effect of it,
The effect of you.
When I took the drug of love,
To fall for you.
Like an enchanting spell,
I couldn't even rebel.
Was it the day my heart fluttered?
Or when you made eye contact.
I didn't knew the effect of it,
The effect of you.
When I took the drug of love,
To fall for you.

15. EASY OR TRICKY

Looking from afar,
You had the eyes like a twinkling star.
Sitting at a bar,
With a magnificent charm.
Describing you from the outside,
It was so easy.
But when I looked inside,
It was all tricky.
Looking from afar,
You had the eyes like a twinkling star.
Sitting at a bar,
With a magnificent charm.
Such a mess of thoughts,
Tensions of all sorts.
Eyes without any fear,
Keeping everyone dear.
Looking from afar,
You had the eyes like a twinkling star.
Sitting at a bar,
With a magnificent charm.

16. ENOUGH THEFT

Seeing you on the tracks,
Waiting for you in the stands,
To finish your game.
Who was the one to blame?
From sharing the books,
Now I'm throwing it toward you.
Was cheating the only option left,
Was my heart not enough theft.
Seeing you on the tracks,
While waiting in the stands,
To finish your game.
Who was the one to blame?
Loving you felt like a game
Where only one player played
Was cheating the only option left,
Was my heart not enough theft.

17. EROS

From one to two,
My soul joined you.
Making a unification,
With lots of communication.
Joining souls,
With the power of love,
I don't ask much,
Let's stay as it was.
I have done my part.
And we know,
Unification is hard,
Without being scarred.
From one to two,
My soul joined you.
Making a unification,
With lots of communication.

18. EVERYTHING RIGHT

Just to do everything right,
I'm here to fight.
I'm putting in all my might,
But the world is no more on my side.
Your eyes are fixated on my face,
I can feel the tension radiate.
I can feel my face turn red,
Without an exchange of words.
Just to do everything right,
I'm here to fight.
I'm putting in all my might,
But the world is no more on my side.
Choosing to fight alone,
I'll conquer the throne.
Where I'll stand above all,
With you across the hall.
Just to do everything right,
I'm here to fight.
I'm putting in all my might,
But the world is no more on my side.

19. EXPECTATION

I am in midst of these noises,
But you are my only choice.
Forgetting about my headache,
I run towards you.
Maybe one day,
you will choose me too.
trying everything new,
and forgetting all the echoes.
I am in midst of these noises,
But you are my only choice.
Forgetting about my headache,
I run towards you.
Expectations of my life,
Starts and ends with you.
Walking hand in hand with you,
Hoping all this becomes true.

20. EYES & LOVE

Eyes shimmering as I see you,
Angry when with someone else!
Softening when talking to you,
Telling you the truth.
Was it the rays of the sun?
The sprinkle of rainwater,
The greenery of the grass,
Or the growing plants?
Expressing my love!
Sneakingly texting you,
or on long calls.
I always imagine ourselves!
Talking and walking,
From winter till fall.
Was it the rays of the sun?
The sprinkle of rainwater,
The greenery of the grass,
Or the growing plants?
Expressing my love!

21. FIGHTING THE MESS

Distant from you,
How will I survive?
Feelings buried in,
And I might just die.
Seated on your stairs,
I'm fighting the mess.
I keep watching,
Where you lie.
The gravestone is grey,
And so is the sky.
Seated on your stairs,
I'm fighting the mess.

22. FROM THE SHELF

Sipping coffee with a bit of honey,
Feet wrapped fuzzy.
Arms all around me,
It is like therapy.
Escaping the reality,
I have met you.
I don't want to go back,
Where I don't have you.
Long winter nights,
Draped in sheets.
Turning the pages,
I meet you.
You bring me back to life,
Just like yourself.
Come back to me another day,
From the shelf!

23. GOOD TIMES

Remembering the good times,
Seeing flashbacks of you.
Thinking of the time when I loved you,
Even when you didn't do it.
Nights of thinking,
Till I meet you.
Long-distance,
Still want to seek you.
Remembering the good times,
Seeing flashbacks of you.
Thinking of the time when I loved you,
Even when you didn't do it.
Sending prayers,
Silently talking on the stairs.
After shedding a few tears,
Sending my heart for repairs.
Remembering the good times,
Seeing flashbacks of you.
Thinking of the time when I loved you,
Even when you didn't do it.

24. GRIM

Drink after drink,
I see the world shrink.
My eyes filled to the brim,
And everyone is grim.
All alone without any support,
With no one to escort.
And no transport,
Life is a maze, in short.
Drink after drink,
I see the world shrink.
My eyes filled to the brim,
And everyone is grim.
Songs running in my ears,
With lanes of tears.
Sitting on the stairs,
Thinking about all the questionnaires.
Drink after drink,
I see the world shrink.
My eyes filled to the brim,
And everyone is grim.

25. GRIPPED

On a busy day,
Find someone to say hey!
Love yourself every day,
Even if your body says not today!
Have a coffee,
Eat a toffee.
It's all about being jolly,
Make your day less foggy.
On a busy day,
Find someone to say hey!
Love yourself every day,
Even if your body says not today!
Find a way to love yourself,
Nobody else is going to do it.
Be the best version of yourself,
Keep your life gripped.

26. HOME

Our love is not easy,
It never was.
We had to be sneaky,
Even how difficult it was.
Without you in here,
It's just a house.
Make it a home,
Stay even if it's a dare.
Each corner misses you,
As my heartbeats.
Was it too good to be true?
Like having double treats!
I just want to see your face,
Feel your embrace.
Maybe one day you'll feel the same,
Till then I'll keep my faith.

27. I WILL MEET YOU

Maybe in another life, I will meet you,
When I will not be so alone.
I'll be walking hand in hand with you,
And I don't have to mourn.
Scenarios in my head,
You are not there.
Maybe we'll make it,
One day away from here.
Maybe in another life, I will meet you,
When I will not be so alone.
I'll be walking hand in hand with you,
And I don't have to mourn.
Reliving the shared moments,
Hoping to see you again,
When I will reach you,
will you be waiting there?

28. IGNORE AND FOCUS

Ignore the people around you,
Focus on yourself.
Eyes may be distracted,
but the mind never lies.
Think of the days,
When the reality was out.
They kept me restrained,
And muffled my shouts.
All they do is lie,
Make a façade.
Always do for the price,
And trade.
Ignore the people around you,
Focus on yourself.
Eyes may be distracted,
but the mind never lies.

29. ILLUSION

It was all an illusion,
With you along my loved one.
I never knew the illusion of,
Caring and loving someone.
Moments with you and
Comfortable silences aren't anymore,
All of it has come to an end,
Just like the cuddling sessions.
It was all an illusion,
With you along my loved one.
I never knew the illusion of,
Caring and loving someone.

30. MERRY-GO-ROUND

Stepping onto the ground,
When life turned into a merry-go-round.
Stumbling on my feet,
When you offered me your seat!
Things falling onto places like snow,
Riverlike eyes overflowed.
Barren hands wiped the tears off,
Even if it was too tough to do.
Stepping onto the ground,
When life turned into a merry-go-round.
Stumbling on my feet,
When you offered me your seat!
Sharing a baguette.
Too good to forget,
When those hesitant eyes,
Tuned soft.

31. JUST A TRY

Laying on my bed, I cry,
Trying to picture the sky.
I'm thinking about you nonstop,
Why is my love a flop?
Tears are falling like raindrops.
Seeing you on all the turns,
Mouth gasping for air like dying.
Is this my fault for trying?
The world that was revolving
around you,
It has crashed somehow!
Maybe it was just a try,
Which made my heart touch the sky!
Tears are falling like raindrops.
Seeing you on all the turns,
Mouth gasping for air like dying.
Is this my fault for trying!

32. LETTER

Creating a mess of words,
Everything is blurry.
When the page turns,
Even if I'm in no hurry.
Every letter reminds me of you,
See how things changed.
Once the lake was blue,
And have not swallowed you.
Creating a mess of words,
Everything is blurry.
When the page turns,
Even if I'm in no hurry.
Every letter reminds me of you!

33. LOVELESS

Ignoring the odd looks,
Watching over a pile of books.
My eyes still sparkle,
Like newly varnished marble.
Is it my way of walking?
Or the talking?
Is this how it feels to be earnest?
Like feeling loveless.
Pursuing my dreams,
Ignoring all the screams,
Of jealousy and hatred.
Keeping my hope sacred.
Is this how it feels to be earnest?
Like feeling loveless.

34. IN THE GARDEN

I follow you around,
I'm like a lost puppy in the garden.
Full of humans but I still choose you,
To be with you.
Only if you felt the same!
Eyes red like a rose,
And a dripping nose.
It's the plan of the faith,
While life is a race.
I follow you around,
I'm like a lost puppy in a garden.
Full of humans but I still choose you,
To be with you.
Only if you felt the same!

35. MUSICAL TONES

Piano keys,
Guitar chords,
Both joined,
Make musical tones.
Playing love songs,
Singing along.
With you,
everything is too good to be true.
Piano keys,
Guitar chords,
Both joined,
Make musical tones.

36. NORTH- SOUTH

Words slipped out of my mouth
Your anger leveled north
With our relationship going south
I hope it was all worth
Ego crushed I laid
Getting flashes
Sweet and bitter moments followed
Tracing scars of vases
Words slipped out of my mouth
Your anger leveled north
With our relationship going south
I hope it was all worth

37. RAINBOWS

As an almost dead flower,
Survives with a bit of rain.
Celebrates with rainbows,
And soil as it grows.
Like a person does,
With a bit of happiness.
Celebrate with family and friends,
And oneself as it grows.
As an almost dead flower,
Survives with a bit of rain.
Celebrates with rainbows,
And soil as it grows.

38. ROSES AND THORNS

Everyone has a friend or foe,
It's all about how we know.
Aware or not we all say hello,
As roses stay with thorns.
Dominant or talkative,
we don't know.
shy or goofy,
we never know.
Unable to see the truth
In Red, white, blue
Aware or not we all say hello,
As roses stay with thorns.

39. SEEDLING TO BLOOMED

Growing like a tree,
Seedling to bloomed.
You made me see,
I was not doomed.
Look what you've done to me,
I'm vibing to a love song.
Sitting in front of a tree,
I feel lovesick all day long.
Growing like a tree,
Seedling to bloomed.
You made me see,
I was not doomed.
It's the magic of love,
deep inside the bones.
Staying even if I turn into stones,
My soul will watch it from the above.
Growing like a tree,
Seedling to bloomed.
You made me see,
I was not doomed.

40. SEESAW

Sitting on a seesaw of life,
With fear in my eyes.
Unable to see you rise,
Waiting for someone to improvise.
Letting the days pass,
While sitting on the grass.
With numerous questions asked,
Seeing you on the cloud, in contrast.
Sitting on a seesaw of life,
With fear in my eyes.
Unable to see you rise,
Waiting for someone to improvise.
Letting the days pass,
Hallway through on a tree branch.
Leveling up till I meet your eyes,
It's my time to touch the skies.

41. SOMEDAY

Words left your mouth.
Them Wrenching my heart away,
Sizzling with the burn,
Maybe Someday this heat will go away.
My eyes are burning with tears,
A few of them streaming away.
It was like a nightmare,
Saying the words that clogged the drain.
Life is no butterflies and pretty skies,
You have to adjust to petty lies.
Words left your mouth.
Them Wrenching my heart away,
Sizzling with the burn,
Maybe Someday this heat will go away.

42. SWIFTY

Changed me like no one else,
Scream like Taylor swift fans,
Look what you made me do.
Different from who you knew!
Never imagined,
In my wildest dreams.
Of how enchanted,
You make me feel.
Only if could,
Be like a willow.
Forget about the bad blood,
And go with the flow.
Changed me like no one else,
Scream like Taylor swift fans,
Look what you made me do.
Different from who you knew!

43. TATTOO

Imprinted all over me,
Just like a tattoo.
Your smile has found my heart,
Too hard to forget from the start.
It's the permanency with no escapism,
So beautiful, yet painful.
Gives the most pleasure
Yet looks sinful
Imprinted all over me,
Just like a tattoo.
Your smile has found my heart,
Too hard to forget from the start.
I don't want to forget,
Not even a bit.
Only if could get a tattoo,
Without facing a taboo.

44. THE WAY TO YOU

As I matched your steps,
In the spring in the fall.
With a few distracting trips,
Just till the food stall.
I found my way to you,
In this life and many more.
I swear to love you,
Till I can count and much more.
From one day to another,
Till winter and summer.
I took the oath,
From life till death.
I found my way to you,
In this life and many more.
I swear to love you,
Till I can count and much more.

45. TRUE OR FALSE

Days and Night I think about you,
Wondering if your promise was true.
Will you come back?
Even if you forgot the track!
I miss those lovely rides,
Me seated on your side.
The breeze coming in through the window,
And your shoulder became my pillow.
Days and Night I think about you,
Wondering if your promise was true.
Will you come back?
Even if you forgot the track!
Crying inside while faking a smile,
Living the new life without you.
You are away from my sight,
But I still hear the laugh.

46. TRUTH OR MYTH

Unaware of the truth,
Blindly following the myth.
Seeing everything differently,
When I met you silently!
With all the ruined hopes of love,
And I don't know the trope.
As if I was standing on a slope,
Falling downwards without a rope.
Unaware of the truth,
Blindly following the myth.
Seeing everything differently,
When I met you silently!
Hand in hand with you,
Even if it's too good to be true.
Unafraid of someone else,
Hoping for anything to make sense.

47. TWENTY- ONE

I don't want to do it anymore,
All of this makes me riled up.
Take me to a seashore,
Or on a hill away up.
All alone away from anyone,
Already twenty-one.
And not wanting to say I am,
It's all about finding the right one.
I don't want to do it anymore,
All of this makes me riled up.
Take me to a seashore,
Or on a hill away up.

48. VALLEY OF EMOTIONS

Loving you in a daze,
Following you in the maze.
Whenever I look at you,
I realize the truth.
I'm in a valley of emotions,
Ugly crying with my eyes swollen.
Laughing till breathing becomes difficult,
Loving till my tummy does summersault.
Lies and truths undistinguished,
False smiles pasted.
I follow your eyes,
Where the beauty lies.
I'm in a valley of emotions,
Ugly crying with my eyes swollen.
Laughing till breathing becomes difficult,
Loving till my tummy does summersault.

49. YOU

It's all gibberish when looking at you,
I have no sense of what I talk about.
I regret all the moments of staring this long,
Still, I want to do it all over again.
It's all about you,
Everything I want to do.
Every time I close my eyes,
I see you...
It's all gibberish when looking at you,
I have no sense of what I talk about.
I regret all the moments of staring this long,
Still, I want to do it all over again.

50. YOUR SWEETHEART

Another day passed,
Just by thinking about you.
Roaming on the road,
Searching for the signs of you.
The society next door is yours,
All your friends are sour.
Still, I want to be your sweetheart,
Sharing my little heart.
Looking at you on my way home,
Seeing you laugh,
Maybe you can share some?
I hope my love wasn't this tough.
The society next door is yours,
All your friends are sour.
Still, I want to be your sweetheart,
Sharing my little heart.

9 798886 673524

Printed by Libri Plureos GmbH in Hamburg,
Germany